LIFE

BY JONNY ZUCKER

ILLUSTRATED BY ANDREW WILDMAN

FULL FLIGHT

Titles in Full Flight 8

Who Are You?	David Orme
3Dee	Danny Pearson
Doom Clone	Melanie Joyce
Too Risky!	Alison Hawes
Wanda Darkstar	Jane A C West
Galactic Games: Sci-Fi Spy Guy	Roger Hurn
Robot Eyes	Jillian Powell
Charlie's Tin	Lynda Gore
Run For Your Life	Jonny Zucker

Badger Publishing Limited
Suite G08, Business & Technology Centre
Bessemer Drive, Stevenage, Hertfordshire SG1 2DX
Telephone: 01438 791037 Fax: 01438 791036
www.badger-publishing.co.uk

Run For Your Life ISBN 978-1-84926-490-7

Badger Publishing would like to thank Jonny Zucker for his help in putting this series together.

Publisher: David Jamieson
Senior Editor: Danny Pearson
Design: Fiona Grant
Illustration: Andrew Wildman

RUN FOR YOUR LIFE

CONTENTS

New words:

fitness
training
imposters
spectators
bizarre
somersault

Main characters:

Joe

Kat

CHAPTER 1

Training

Joe loved running. He was very fast. He always won all of the races on sports day.

His best friend Kat was his coach. She believed he was good enough to make it to the Olympic Games when he was older.

She read lots of stuff about fitness and training and when he practised his running in the park, she always timed him. They were a good team.

One Saturday they had spent a lot of time in the park. Joe had run well.

He and Kat were talking about their school's sports day. It was in two weeks.

"I think you will win every race this year!" grinned Kat.

As they walked down Track Street, Kat spotted something on the ground. It was an old blank DVD case.

She picked it up. Inside was a DVD. Again, it had no writing on it.

"I wonder what it is," said Joe.

"There's only one way to find out," replied Kat.

Back at Kat's house, they loaded the DVD. Instantly, pictures of people running and jumping and throwing things appeared on the screen.
But they were not wearing modern sports clothes.

They were wearing very old-fashioned clothes.

She grabbed a torch and shone it on the case, looking to see if there were any faded words. But there weren't.

“It must be a film about the ancient Greek Olympics,” said Joe.

“But there are no words,” replied Kat, “and it doesn’t seem like a film - it looks too real.”

Before they could speak again, the picture went blurry and suddenly they felt themselves being pulled forward towards the screen at amazing speed.

“WHAT’S GOING ON?” yelled Joe.

“I DON’T KNOW!” shouted back Kat.

CHAPTER 2
Olympia

A second later they landed with a bump. All sign of Kat's house and her TV had gone.

They were sitting on a stone floor in a small room.

In the middle of the room was a table with some white robes on top of it.

Outside they could hear cheering and shouting.

They stepped out of the room and found themselves in a corridor.

They had only taken three steps, when a large guard holding a sword and shield, blocked their way.

“Er...where are we?” asked Joe.

“You are in Olympia!” cried the guard.

“OLYMPIA?” gasped Joe.

“Yes,” nodded the guard. “The very first Olympic games have just started.”

Kat and Joe gazed at him in awe.

“But you will have to miss the games,” said the guard.

"Why?" asked Joe.

"Because you are going to be fed to the lions!"

"WHAT?" cried Kat.

"Look at the way you are dressed," said the guard. "I have never seen clothes like that! You are imposters so you shall be fed to the lions!"

"Hang on a second," said Kat. "Don't you know who this is?"

She pointed at Joe.

The guard shook his head.

"This is Joe... Josephus!" said Kat. "He is here for the sprint race. We have come from very far away to be here. That is why we have strange clothes."

"I have not heard your name before," frowned the guard, looking at Joe.

"He does not like to boast," said Kat.

The guard thought about this. "OK" he nodded, "you can join the race. If you win, you go free. If you lose, the lions get you."

"That's not fair!" cried Kat.

"It's that or nothing!" barked the guard.

"I will do it," said Joe.

"Good!" said the guard, "I will take you to the other runners."

"Where are they?" asked Kat.

"You cannot come with us," said the guard to Kat. "It is for males only. You must go to the stands and join the spectators."

Kat sighed with disappointment, patted Joe on the shoulder and left.

Joe was now alone with the guard.

CHAPTER 3
Josephus

The guard led Joe down a long passage, past a room where a feast was going on and down some stone steps.

He stopped when they reached an archway.

Through the archway were ten large Greek men, wearing a type of light brown shorts and brown vests.

“This is Josephus!” announced the guard. “He is running in your race.”

The ten men turned round and looked at Joe.

"HIM!" cried the biggest of them.

"Yes, Flavelus, him!" answered the guard.

Flavelus threw back his head and screamed with laughter. “Welcome little Josephus!” he said in a mocking tone. “You will not stand a chance in this race! You will be crushed like a fly!”

The other nine men roared with laughter.

“I will leave him with you,” said the guard.

Nine of the men started doing stretches and exercises, but Flavelus walked over to Joe. He lowered his head towards Joe’s.

“Let me make one thing clear little man,” said Flavelus. “I will win this race and you will be a long way behind me. Do you understand?”

“I thought you said I don’t stand a chance in this race,” replied Joe, sounding a lot braver than he felt.

“Don’t be cheeky!” sneered Flavelus. “Now stay out of my way, and stay well behind me in the race!”

CHAPTER 4

Olympic Arena

Joe stayed well away from Flavelus while he did his warm up exercises.

Twenty minutes later, the guard told the runners that the race was about to begin.

“Remember what I said!” hissed Flavelus in Joe’s face as the runners followed the guard down the corridor.

A few minutes later they walked out into the sunshine of the Olympic arena.

They were met with cheers and applause.

When Joe came out, there was suddenly silence. Who was this boy runner and why were his clothes so bizarre?

An old man in a robe told the runners where to stand on the starting line. This was a line of chalk marked on the ground.

Joe looked down the track. It was about the same length as a modern 100 metres race.

Joe was told to line up next to Flavelus. Flavelus gave him a filthy stare.

The man in the robe raised his right hand in the air. The runners got ready.

The man then threw down his hand.

The race was on!

Joe sprinted forward at electric pace. Even though the other runners were much bigger than him, he knew he could beat them.

He blocked out the great noise of the spectators and flew forwards.

At the race's halfway point he was in the lead.

He kicked his heels and sped up. The race was his to win!

But suddenly, he felt a shot of pain in his left foot.

He looked sideways.

Flavelus had stamped on him. Joe felt himself go tumbling towards the ground.

Disaster! He would be going to the lions!

CHAPTER 5

Finish Line

But instead of falling, Joe managed to do a somersault and land on his feet.

But thanks to his cheating, Flavelus was now ahead of Joe, with the finish line in sight.

It would not be possible to catch Flavelus.

But then something incredible happened. Flavelus suddenly clutched his eyes, stumbled to the left and went crashing onto the ground.

Joe sprinted on and finished the race... in first place!

The old man in the robe strode over to him and placed a gold medal around his neck.

"You are the first ever Olympic winner!" cried the man.

"HOW DARE YOU?" yelled a voice.

It was Flavelus. He was now on his feet, racing towards Joe.

Joe raced back inside the building and had just reached the corridor, when Kat joined him.

"We have to get out of here!" shouted Kat.

"YOU ARE FOR THE LIONS!" screamed Flavelus, sprinting to catch them up and shaking his fists.

Joe and Kat raced into the room they'd arrived in and felt themselves being pulled forward at incredible speed.

A few seconds later they were back in Kat's house.

"What happened to Flavelus in the race?" asked Joe.

Kat reached into her pocket and pulled out her torch. "I shone it straight into his eyes and it blinded him for a second!" she grinned.

"You are a genius!" shouted Joe.

The next day in school, Kat and Joe's class were studying the ancient Greeks.

The class turned to a page about the very first Olympic games.

"Look at that!" cried someone. "That guy in the race looks just like Joe."

"And there's a girl in the crowd that looks like Kat!" said someone else.

"Very funny!" laughed the teacher, "now let's move on."

Joe and Kat exchanged a glance, but neither of them said anything.

OLYMPIC GAMES

- *'The Olympic Games are a major international event in which thousands of athletes take part.'*
- *The first ever Olympic Games were held in 776 BC in Olympia.*
- *The Greeks referred to the event as the 'Olympiad.'*
- *They held the games every 4 years, exactly the same as today.*

- *The games ran until AD 391.*
- *A temple on the site of Olympia was dedicated to the Greek god, Zeuss.*
- *The Olympic Games were started again in Athens in 1896.*

QUESTIONS

- *In what ways did Kat help Joe with his running?*
- *What was strange about the DVD and its case?*
- *What reason does the guard give for throwing them to the lions?*
- *How does Flavelus first react to Joe?*
- *In what way does Flavelus cheat in the race?*
- *How is Flavelus made to fall?*